GRANDMA'S FAVOURITES

CAKES & PUDDINGS

MARGARET KEENAN

Published in 2010 by TAJ Books International LLP

27, Ferndown Gardens,
Cobham,
Surrey,
UK,
KT11 2BH

www.tajbooks.com

ISBN-13: 978-1-84406-164-8

Printed in China.

CONTENTS

ALMOND AND CHERRY CHEESECAKE

Metric	Ingredient	Imperial
128 g	ground almonds	1 cup
43 g	graham cracker crumbs	1/3 cup
32 g	butter, melted	1/4 cup
226 g	cream cheese, softened	8 oz
400 ml	sweetened condensed milk	14 fl oz
	3 eggs	
600 g	cherry pie filling, divided	21 oz

Method

1. In a small bowl, combine almonds and cracker crumbs; stir in butter. Press onto the bottom of a greased 9-in. springform pan; set aside. In a bowl, beat the cream cheese and milk until smooth. Add eggs, beat on low just until combined. Pour into prepared crust.

2. Refrigerate 1/2 cup pie filling for garnish. Drop remaining pie filling by teaspoonfuls onto cream cheese mixture; cut through batter with a knife to swirl the filling. Bake at 170 ° C/325 ° F/Gas Mark 3 for 50-55 minutes or until center is almost set. Cool on a wire rack for 10 minutes. Carefully run a knife around edge of pan to loosen; cool 1 hour longer. Chill overnight. Remove sides of pan. Cut cheesecake into slices; garnish with reserved pie filling. Refrigerate leftovers. Yield: 12 servings.

ANGEL CAKE

Metric	Ingredient	Imperial
115 g	plain flour	4 oz
85 g	icing sugar	3 oz
	8 large egg whites, at room temperature	
150 g	caster sugar	5 1/2 oz
	1/4 tsp salt	
	(To serve)	
225 g	strawberries, cut into quarters	8 oz
225 g	raspberries	8 oz
225 g	blueberries	8 oz
300 g	fromage frais	10 1/2 oz

Method

1. Preheat the oven to 180 ° C/350 ° F/Gas Mark 4. Sift the flour and icing sugar onto a large plate and set aside.

2. Put the egg whites in a large bowl and whisk until quite frothy. Add the sugar, salt, cream of tartar and vanilla extract, and continue whisking until the mixture forms stiff peaks.

3. Sift the flour mixture over the egg whites and fold in very gently with a large metal spoon until well blended.

4. Spoon the mixture into an ungreased 25 cm (10 in) non-stick tube tin, making sure there are no air pockets. Bake for 35 minutes or until well risen, golden brown and springy to the touch.

5. Invert the cake, still in the tin, onto a wire rack and leave to cool completely, upside down. When it is cold, slide a long knife around the side of the tin to loosen the cake, then invert it onto a serving plate. (The cake can be kept, wrapped in cling film or stored in an airtight container, for 1–2 days.)

6. Just before serving, mix together the strawberries, raspberries and blueberries. Spoon the fruit into the hollow in the centre of the cake. Serve with the fromage frais in a bowl.

ALMOND AND ORANGE CAKE

Metric	Ingredient	Imperial
	2 large navel oranges, (choose oranges with unblemished skins as the whole fruit is used in this recipe)	
	5 eggs	
250 g	caster sugar	1 1/4 cups
250 g	ground almonds	2 1/2 cups
	1 tsp gluten-free baking powder	
	Pure icing sugar to serve	

Method

1. **Preheat oven to** 170 ° C/325 ° F/Gas Mark 3. Grease and line the base of a heart-shaped pan.

2. **Place the two whole** oranges in a saucepan and cover with water. Bring to the boil and simmer, covered, for 1 hour, ensuring that the oranges remain covered with water. Drain and cool. Chop the oranges into quarters, discard any seeds, then place the chunks into a blender and puree until smooth.

3. **Beat the eggs with** the sugar until thick, then add the orange puree, ground almonds and baking powder and mix well.

4. **Pour into prepared pan** and bake for 1 hour. Leave the cake to firm up in the pan for 20 minutes then turn out, remove the baking paper and turn over to finish cooling right way up. This cake definitely mellows with a little time and can be prepared up to 48 hours in advance.

5. **To serve, sift icing** sugar on top and decorate with orange zest and almonds.

ANGEL CAKE

Metric	Ingredient	Imperial
115 g	plain flour	4 oz
85 g	icing sugar	3 oz
	8 large egg whites, at room temperature	
150 g	caster sugar	5 1/2 oz
	1/4 tsp salt	
	(To serve)	
225 g	strawberries, cut into quarters	8 oz
225 g	raspberries	8 oz
225 g	blueberries	8 oz
300 g	fromage frais	10 1/2 oz

Method

1. **Preheat the oven to** 180 ° C/350 ° F/Gas Mark 4. Sift the flour and icing sugar onto a large plate and set aside.

2. **Put the egg whites** in a large bowl and whisk until quite frothy. Add the sugar, salt, cream of tartar and vanilla extract, and continue whisking until the mixture forms stiff peaks.

3. **Sift the flour mixture** over the egg whites and fold in very gently with a large metal spoon until well blended.

4. **Spoon the mixture into** an ungreased 25 cm (10 in) non-stick tube tin, making sure there are no air pockets. Bake for 35 minutes or until well risen, golden brown and springy to the touch.

5. **Invert the cake, still** in the tin, onto a wire rack and leave to cool completely, upside down. When it is cold, slide a long knife around the side of the tin to loosen the cake, then invert it onto a serving plate. (The cake can be kept, wrapped in cling film or stored in an airtight container, for 1–2 days.)

6. **Just before serving, mix** together the strawberries, raspberries and blueberries. Spoon the fruit into the hollow in the centre of the cake. Serve with the fromage frais in a bowl.

APPLE CRUMBLE

Metric	Ingredient	Imperial
	(for the crumble)	
300 g	plain flour, sieved pinch of salt	10 1/2 oz
175 g	unrefined brown sugar	6 oz
200 g	unsalted butter, cubed at room temperature	7oz
	Knob of butter for greasing	
	(for the filling)	
450 g	apples, peeled, cored and cut into 1cm/½in pieces	1 lb
50 g	unrefined brown sugar	2 oz
	1 tbsp plain flour	
	1 pinch of ground cinnamon	

Method

1. Preheat the oven to 180 ° C/350 ° F/Gas Mark 4.

2. Place the flour and sugar in a large bowl and mix well. Taking a few cubes of butter at a time rub into the flour mixture. Keep rubbing until the mixture resembles breadcrumbs.

3. Place the fruit in a large bowl and sprinkle over the sugar, flour and cinnamon. Stir well being careful not to break up the fruit.

4. Butter a 24cm/9in ovenproof dish. Spoon the fruit mixture into the bottom, then sprinkle the crumble mixture on top.

5. Bake in the oven for 40-45 minutes until the crumble is browned and the fruit mixture bubbling.

6. Serve with thick cream or custard.

APPLE AND JAM PUFF PASTRY

Metric	Ingredient	Imperial
	1 sheet frozen puff pastry, thawed	
	2 Granny Smith apples or two peaches, peeled, cored and sliced paper thin	
110 g	apricot jam or preserves	1/2 cup
75 g	brown sugar	1/3 cup
	1/2 tsp cinnamon	
110 g	chopped pistachios	1/2 cup

Method

1. **Roll pastry onto a** well floured surface into a 12" x 12" rectangle and cut into nine 3" squares.

2. **Prick the pastry with** a fork and coat each with a spoonful of apricot jam. Fan the apple slices over the jam, arranged nicely.

3. **In small bowl, combine** brown sugar and cinnamon and mix well. Sprinkle over apple (or peach) slices. Put the tarts on an ungreased cookie sheet.

4. **Bake at 180 ° C/350 ° F/Gas Mark 4** for 10-12 minutes, until the apple slices are crisp-tender and the pastry is golden brown. Sprinkle with pistachios.

APPLE STRUDEL

Metric	Ingredient	Imperial
680 g	eating apples, peeled, cored and chopped	1 1/2 lbs
	1/2 orange, juice and zest only	
100 g	caster sugar	3 1/2 oz
	freshly grated nutmeg, to taste	
55 g	sultanas	2 oz
	6-8 sheets ready-made filo pastry	
55 g	butter, melted and cooled, plus extra for greasing	2 oz
	2 tbsp dried breadcrumbs	

Method

1. **Preheat the oven to** 190 ° C/375 ° F/Gas Mark 5.

2. **Place the apple, orange** juice and zest, sugar, nutmeg and sultanas into a large bowl and mix well.

3. **Brush each sheet of** filo pastry with melted butter, then place the sheets of pastry on top of each other onto a large sheet of greaseproof paper.

4. **Sprinkle the top sheet** of filo with some dried breadcrumbs, then spoon the apple mixture down the middle of the filo sheet.

5. **Carefully roll the pastry** up around the filling like a cigar, using the greaseproof paper to help.

6. **Place the filo roll** onto a greased baking tray, brush with any remaining melted butter and cook for 30-40 minutes, until lightly browned and the filling is hot.

BANANA CAKE

Metric	Ingredient	Imperial
	2 ripe bananas (overipe is best)	
170 g	caster sugar	6 oz
170 g	self raising flour	6 oz
170 g	soft margarine	6 oz
	3 eggs	
	Few drops vanilla essence	

Method

1. **Use a food processor** Pre heat oven to 170 ° C/325 ° F/Gas Mark 3

2. **Add all ingredients and** blend until well mixed

3. **Pour into lined loaf** tin

4. **Bake for 1 hour**

5. **Cool and enjoy**

6. **If you are a** nut lover, once ingredients are blended add 60g chopped walnuts and blend in to the mixture

BANOFFEE PIE

Metric	Ingredient	Imperial
300 g	oaty biscuits (Hob Nobs are good)	10 1/2 oz
60 g	butter, melted	2 oz
397 g	tin Nestlé Carnation Caramel	14 oz
	3 large bananas , sliced	
350 ml	double cream	12 fl oz
	1 tbsp icing sugar	
100 g	dark chocolate	3 1/2 oz

Method

1. **Heat the oven to** 180 ° C/350 ° F/Gas Mark 4.

2. **Crush the biscuits in** a food processor then add the melted butter and pulse to combine. Press the mixture into a 24cm tart tin, with a removable base, in an even layer.

3. **Transfer the tin to** a baking sheet and cook for 10-12 minutes, until lightly toasted and set. Leave to cool then gently release from the tin and put on a serving plate.

4. **Spread the caramel over** the biscuit base and chill for 1 hour. Arrange the banana slices over the toffee. Whip the cream and sugar together to form soft peaks and spread over the bananas. melt the chocolate in a microwave or in a bowl set over, not in, a pan of simmering water.

5. **Allow to cool slightly,** before drizzling over the cream.

BREAD AND BUTTER PUDDING

Metric	Ingredient	Imperial
25 g	butter, plus extra for greasing	1 oz
	8 thin slices bread	
50 g	sultanas	2 oz
	2 tsp cinnamon powder	
350 ml	whole milk	12 fl oz
50 ml	double cream	2 fl oz
	2 free-range eggs	
25 g	granulated sugar	1 oz
	nutmeg, grated, to taste	

Method

1. **Grease a 1 litre/2** pint pie dish with butter.

2. **Cut the crusts off** the bread. Spread each slice with on one side with butter, then cut into triangles.

3. **Arrange a layer of** bread, buttered-side up, in the bottom of the dish, then add a layer of sultanas. Sprinkle with a little cinnamon, then repeat the layers of bread and sultanas, sprinkling with cinnamon, until you have used up all of the bread. Finish with a layer of bread, then set aside.

4. **Gently warm the milk** in a pan over a low heat to scalding point. Don't let it boil.

5. **Crack the eggs into** a bowl, add three quarters of the sugar and lightly whisk until pale.

6. **Add the warm milk** and cream mixture and stir well, then strain the custard into a bowl.

7. **Pour the custard over** the prepared bread layers and sprinkle with nutmeg and the remaining sugar and leave to stand for 30 minutes.

8. **Preheat the oven to** 180 ° C/355 ° F/Gas Mark 4. Place the dish into the oven and bake for 30-40 minutes, or until the custard has set and the top is golden-brown.

CANNOLI

Metric	Ingredient	Imperial
250 g	plain flour	9 oz
	1 tsp cocoa powder	
	1 tsp coffee, freshly ground	
30 g	butter, softened	1 oz
25 g	sugar	1 oz
60 ml	white wine	2 fl oz
	1 egg, beaten	
	olive oil, for deep-frying	
	icing sugar, to decorate	
	(for the filling)	
600 g	ricotta cheese	21 oz
150 g	icing sugar	5 1/3 oz
25 g	chocolate chips	1oz
50 g	candied fruits, finely chopped	1 1/2 oz

Method

1. **First make the filling.** Place ricotta and icing sugar in a large bowl and whisk until creamy. Fold in the chocolate chips and candied fruits. Set aside.

2. **To make the pastry,** place the flour, cocoa powder, coffee, butter and sugar in a large bowl and mix well together. Gradually add the wine and mix well until the mixture forms pastry dough. Form the pastry into a ball and wrap in cling film. Leave to rest for an hour.

3. **Lightly flour a clean** work surface and roll out the pastry to a thickness of about 3mm. With a round pastry cutter, cut circles with a diameter of about 7.5 cm and wrap around the tubular moulds, securing the edges with the beaten egg.

4. **Heat the olive oil** in a large pan to 180 ° C/350 ° F. Fry the cannoli until golden-brown. Drain on kitchen paper and gently remove the moulds.

5. **Leave to cool, and** then fill the cannoli with the ricotta mixture. Sprinkle with icing sugar and serve.

CARAMEL CUSTARD

Metric	Ingredient	Imperial
60 g	granulated sugar	1/4 cup
750 ml	scalded milk	3 cups
	4 beaten eggs	
60 g	granulated sugar	1/4 cup
	1/2 tsp vanilla	

Method

1. Butter 6 custard cups.

2. Melt 1/4 cup of sugar in a small heavy skillet, stirring constantly, until a caramel syrup forms; pour immediately into prepared custard cups.

3. Add a small amount of the hot milk to beaten eggs, stirring briskly.

4. Add remaining milk; add 1/4 cup sugar and the vanilla; blend well. Pour mixture into custard cups.

5. Set cups in a large, shallow baking pan in a 170 ° C/325° F/Gas Mark 3 oven. Pour hot water into the large baking pan to a depth of about 1 inch. Bake for about 45 minutes, or until a knife inserted in center comes out clean.

6. Unmold into shallow dessert dishes to serve.

CARROT AND APRICOT CAKE

Metric	Ingredient	Imperial
	4 medium eggs	
175 g	light soft brown sugar	6 oz
150 ml	sunflower oil	5 fl oz
200 g	self-raising flour	7 oz
300 g	carrots, grated	10 oz
	1tsp mixed spices	
75 g	dried apricots, finely chopped	2 1/2 oz
25 g	raisins	1 oz

Method

1. **Preheat the oven to** 180 º C/350 º C/Gas Mark 4. Take a 2lb loaf tin, and grease and base-line it with baking paper.

2. **Crack the eggs into** a large bowl, add the sugar and whisk until thick and creamy, then gradually whisk in the sunflower oil.

3. **Sieve the flour into** the whisked mixture and gently fold together. Add the rest of the ingredients and carefully mix everything together.

4. **Spoon mixture into the** tin. Level the surface and bake for 45 to 50 minutes, until firm to touch and golden brown (check after 35 minutes and cover the top if it's getting too brown). Dust with icing sugar to serve.

CHARLOTTE CAKE WITH STRAWBERRY

Metric	Ingredient	Imperial
	2 envelopes Unflavored Gelatine	
180 g	sugar, divided	3/4 cup
	1/4 tsp salt	
	4 eggs, separated	
113 g	water	1/2 cup
570 g	strawberries	20 oz
	2 tbsp lemon juice	
	2 tsp grated lemon rind	
	8 Lady Fingers	
236 ml	heavy cream, whipped	1 cup

Method

1. Mix gelatine, 1/4 cup of the sugar and salt thoroughly in top of a double boiler

2. Beat egg yolks and water together. Add to gelatine mixture. Add 1 package of the frozen sliced strawberries (or divided fresh strawberry equivalent)

3. Cook over boiling water, stirring constantly until gelatine is dissolved and straberries thawed, about 8 minutes.

4. Remove from heat and add remaining package of strawberries, lemon juice and rind. Stir until berries are thawed.

5. Chill in refrigerator or in bowl of ice and water, stirring occasionally, until the mixture mounds when dropped from spoon.

6. Split Lady Fingers in half and stand around edge of an 8-inch spring form pan.

7. Beat egg whites until stiff. Beat in remaining 1/2 cup sugar. Fold in gelatine mixture.

8. Fold in whipped cream. Turn into pan and chill until firm.

9. Remove from pan and garnish with additional whipped cream and strawberries, or garnishes of your choice.

CHERRY CHEESECAKE

Metric	Ingredient	Imperial
	(for the base)	
175 g	digestive biscuits	6 oz
	2 level tsp light soft brown sugar	
30 g	butter, melted	1 oz
	(for the filling)	
300 g	full-fat soft cheese	
150 g	caster sugar	5 oz
	Finely grated rind and juice 1 lemon	
142 ml	double cream	5 fl oz
	sachet powdered gelatine	
	2 medium egg whites	
	(for the topping)	
350 g	cherries, stoned	12 oz
	6 level tbsp caster sugar	
	1 level tbsp arrowroot	

Method

1. **To make the base:** Crush the biscuits and stir in the brown sugar and melted butter, or whizz the ingredients together in a food processor. Press the mixture into the base of the lined tin and chill it until firm.

2. **To make the filling:** Beat together the soft cheese, caster sugar and lemon rind and juice. Lightly whip the cream and fold it into the cheese mixture. Sprinkle the gelatine over 4tbsp water in a bowl and leave it to sponge for a few minutes, then dissolve it either in a microwave oven or over a pan of hot water. Whisk the egg whites until firm. Working quickly, before the gelatine sets, fold the gelatine into the cheese mixture and fold in the egg whites. Pour the mixture over the biscuit base and spread out to level the top. Chill until filling is firm.

3. **To make the topping:** Pour 150ml (1/4 pint) water into a pan and add the cherries and caster sugar. Bring to a gentle boil and simmer for 1-2 minutes until the cherries are just tender. Blend the arrowroot with 2tbsp water and add to the pan, stirring well so that the juices thicken. Simmer for 1-2 minutes, then remove the pan from the heat and leave the cherries to cool.

4. **Remove the cheesecake from** the tin and peel away the lining paper and transfer it to a serving plate. Spoon the cherry mixture on top and serve.

CHERRY CRUMBLE CAKE

Metric	Ingredient	Imperial
300 g	soft unsalted butter	10 oz
500 g	morello cherries, out of a jar and drained	17 oz
225 g	caster sugar	8 oz
500 g	plain flour	17 oz
	1 tsp baking powder	
	1/2 tsp zest of an unwaxed lemon	
	1 tsp cinnamon	
	1 egg	
	2 tbsp ground almonds	
	salt	

Method

1. **Preheat the oven to** 200 ° C/400 ° F/Gas Mark 6. Grease a 26 cm springform cake tin.

2. **To make the crumble,** sift the plain flour and baking powder in a mixing bowl, add sugar, lemon zest, cinnamon, egg, softened butter and a pinch of salt. Whisk, with a kneading hook, until the crumble has the right texture.

3. **Use 1/2 of the** crumble to line the base of the springform tin and press firmly together. Sprinkle with the almonds and spread the cherries, then spread the remaining crumble mixture over the cherries. Bake for 35-40 minutes until golden brown.

4. **Leave the cake in** the tin for about 15 minutes. Then loosen the edges of the cake with a knife and carefully remove the ring. Loosen the base of the cake to detach it from the base of the springform tin do not remove the entire springform cake tin. Put on a wire rack to cool down still leaving it inside the springform.

CHOCOLATE CAKE

Metric	Ingredient	Imperial
175 g	margarine or softened butter	6 oz
175 g	caster sugar	6 oz
	3 large eggs	
150 g	self-raising flour, sifted	5 oz
50 g	cocoa, sifted	1 3/4 oz
	1tsp baking powder	
	1tsp vanilla extract	
	pinch of salt	
	(for simple chocolate icing)	
100 g	dark chocolate	3 1/2 oz
100 g	chopped butter	3 1/2 oz

Method

1. Heat the oven to 180 ° C/350 ° F/Gas Mark 4. Lightly grease an 18cm (7in) round cake tin with a little extra butter or margarine and cut a piece of greaseproof paper or non-stick baking parchment to fit the base of the tin.

2. Put all the ingredients in a large mixing bowl and beat with a wooden spoon or a hand-held mixer for 1 minute, or until just combined. It's important not to beat the batter too much just long enough to make it smooth.

3. Pour or spoon the mixture into the tin, smooth the top and bake on the middle shelf of the oven for about 45-50 minutes. The cake is cooked when it looks well risen and golden; the top should spring back when lightly touched with a fingertip. Another test is to insert a skewer into the centre of the cake - it should come out clean.

4. Let the cake sit in the tin for 5 minutes, then gently run a knife around the edge and turn the cake out onto a wire rack to cool.

5. For the icing, place the dark chocolate and chopped butter in a heatproof bowl and set over a saucepan of very hot water until melted. Cool for 15 minutes, then spread over the top of the cooled cake.

CHOCOLATE ECLAIR

Metric	Ingredient	Imperial	Metric	Ingredient	Imperial
	(for the choux pastry)			3 drops vanilla extract	
125 ml	water	4 fl oz		2 tsp caster sugar	
50 g	butter	1 3/4 oz		(for the icing)	
60 g	plain flour	2 oz	50 g	dark chocolate, chopped	1 3/4 oz
	2 eggs, beaten			1 tsp butter	
	(for the filling)			2 tbsp water	
300 ml	double cream	10 fl oz	85 g	icing sugar	3 oz

Method

1. For the choux pastry, pour the water into a medium saucepan and add the butter. Place the pan over a medium heat, and as soon as the butter melts, turn up the heat and bring to a boil. Shoot in all the flour in one go and take the pan off the heat.

2. Stir briskly until the flour has blended in with the liquid and the mixture leaves the sides of the pan and makes a soft ball. It's best not to overbeat at this stage otherwise you'll end up with heavy pastry. Preheat the oven to 200 °C/400 ° F/Gas Mark 6.

3. Leave the mixture to cool slightly, and then start beating in the eggs, a tablespoon at a time. Beat well between each addition - the more air you can incorporate, the lighter the pastry. Spoon the paste into a piping bag fitted with a 1cm plain nozzle and pipe finger lengths, about 5cm long onto a lightly oiled and floured baking tray. Leave about 3cm space between each eclair, as they need space to puff up in the oven.

4. Bake the eclairs for about 20 minutes before turning down the heat to 190 ° C/375 ° F/Gas Mark 5 for another 10 minutes. They should be golden brown and well-risen. Remove from the oven and pierce each éclair with a trussing needle or the point of a sharp knife, so that the steam can escape without making the pastry soggy. Leave to cool on a wire rack.

5. Whip the cream with the vanilla and sugar, and spoon into a clean piping bag fitted with a plain nozzle. Widen the hole made by the trussing needle and insert the piping nozzle. Pipe the cream into the éclairs and place in the fridge to firm up while you make the icing.

6. Tip the chocolate into a heatproof bowl and add the butter and water. Place over a saucepan of simmering water and stir until melted. Add the sieved icing sugar, a little at a time. With a palette knife, smooth the icing over the top of each éclair and leave on one side until set.

7. If you don't fancy piping the choux pastry, you can spoon rough heaps onto a baking sheet instead and make profiteroles instead.

CHOCOLATE MOCHA CAKE

Metric	Ingredient	Imperial
320 g	cake flour (not self-rising)	2 1/2 cup
	2 tsp baking soda	
	1/2 tsp salt	
235 ml	vegetable oil	1 cup
235 ml	buttermilk	1 cup
225 g	sugar	1 3/4 cup
	3 large eggs, at room temperature	
64 g	cocoa powder	1/2 cup
	(for the frosting)	
96 g	unsalted butter, softened to room temperature	3/4 cup
450 g	confectioner's powdered sugar	1 lb
30 g	cocoa powder	1/4 cup
40 g	cooled espresso or strong coffee	1/3 cup

Method

1. **Preheat over to 350** ° C/180 ° F/Gas Mark 4. Lightly grease two 9 x 1 1/2 inch layer cake pans; dust lightly with flour; tap out any excess. On waxed paper sift together flour, baking soda and salt. In 2 cup glass measure combine vegetable oil and buttermilk.

2. **In large bowl with** electric mixer at high speed, beat sugar and eggs until light and fluffy. At low speed, blend in cocoa. Beat in flour mixture alternately with buttermilk mixture, beating after each addition until smooth and creamy. Scrape sides of bowl down with rubber scraper after each addition. Pour batter into prepared pans.

3. **Bake 30 to 35** minutes or until the centers spring back when they are lightly pressed with fingertip or a wooden pick inserted in center comes out clean. Cool layers in pans on wire racks 15 minutes; loosen around edges with knife; turn out onto wire racks; cool completely. Put layers together with Chocolate Mocha Frosting; frost sides and top with remaining frosting. Makes one 9 inch two-layer cake.

4. **For the mocha frosting:** In large bowl with electric mixer at medium speed, beat butter until fluffy-light. At low speed, add sugar and cocoa powder alternately with cooled espresso or coffee until creamy-smooth. Use to fill and frost Chocolate Cake. Makes 2 1/2 cups.

CLEMENTINE CAKE

Metric	Ingredient	Imperial
	2 clementine oranges	
175 g	softened butter	6 oz
175 g	caster sugar	6 oz
	3 eggs, beaten	
175 g	self-raising flour	6 oz
	4 tbsp ground almonds	
	3 tbsp yoghurt	
	1 tbsp clementine juice	
	(for the glaze and topping)	
	6 tbsp clementine juice	
	2 tbsp caster sugar	
	3 white sugar cubes, crushed	

Method

1. **Grease a cake tin** and line the bottom with baking parchment. Then pare the rind from the clementines and chop finely (alternatively grate the rind. For extra zing, add the rind of a lemon quarter).

2. **In a bowl, cream** together the butter, sugar, and clementine rind until the mix is pale and fluffy. Gradually add the beaten eggs, mixing well after each addition. Then gently fold-in the self-raising flour, followed by the ground almonds, cream and clementine juice. Spoon the mixture into the prepared tin and smooth the surface. Bake in a preheated oven at 180 ° C/350 ° C/Gas Mark 4 for about 55 minutes, or until a fine skewer inserted into its centre comes out clean. Leave on one side to cool, and prepare the glaze.

3. **In a small saucepan,** add the clementine juice and sugar, bringing the mix to the boil. Simmer for five minutes and drizzle over the cake until it has been absorbed, then sprinkle with crushed sugar cubes.

COFFEE CAKE

Metric	Ingredient	Imperial
150 g	caster sugar	5 oz
150 g	butter or margarine	5 oz
	3 eggs	
150 g	self raising flour	5 oz
	1 1/2 tsp baking powder	
	1 tbsp hot water	
	1 tbsp instant coffee	
	(for The icing)	
225 g	icing sugar	8 oz
100 g	butter or margarine	3 1/2 oz
	1 1/2 tbsp instant coffee	
	1 tbsp hot water	
	Strawberry jam (optional)	

Method

1. **Preheat the oven at** 160 ° C/325 ° F/Gas Mark 3.Baseline and grease two equally sized sandwich tins. Add the sugar and the butter to a bowl and whisk until very fluffy and a pale cream.

2. **Wisk the eggs in** a mug with a fork and then add them gradually to the mixture with 1 tbsp of flour each time. Make sure you don't use all the flour. Add the rest of the flour and the baking powder to the mixture and fold it in gently.

4. **Dissolve the coffee in** the boiling water and add to the mixture still folding. Divide into the sandwich tins and cook for 30 minutes

5. **Meanwhile Cream the butter** and the icing sugar until light and fluffy. Dissolve the coffee in boiling water, making sure you don't add too much water or the icing will be runny and add it to the butter and icing sugar. Whisk and leave in the fridge until the cake is done.

6. **Once the cakes are** done and have been put onto plates spread the icing on the bottom of one of the cakes (leaving around half of the icing for the top) and spread the strawberry jam onto the bottom of the other. Spread the remainig icing ontop of the cake. decorate with cherries or walnuts.

CREAM HORN

Metric	Ingredient	Imperial
100 g	puff pastry	4 oz
	beaten egg to glaze	
	raspberry jam	
150 ml	double cream	2/3 cup
75 ml	single cream	3 fl oz
	icing sugar (confectioners sugar) to dredge	

Method

1. Roll out the pastry to a strip measuring 66 x 10 - 11.5 cm (26 x 4 - 4 1/2 inches). Cut the pastry lengthways into 1-cm (1/2-inch) ribbons with a sharp knife.

2. Moisten one edge of each strip and wind each round a cream horn tin starting at the tip, overlapping 0.3 cm (1/4 inch), and finishing neatly on the underside. The pastry should not overlap the metal rim. Brush with beaten egg to glaze.

3. Arrange the cream horns on a dampened baking sheet, join-side down.

4. Bake in the oven at 220 ° C/425 ° F/Gas Mark 7 for 10 minutes until golden brown.

5. Cool for a few minutes then carefully twist each tin, holding the pastry lightly in the other hand to ease it out of the pastry horn.

6. When cold, fill the tip of each horn with a little jam. Whisk the two creams together until stiff and fill the horns down to the jam. Dredge with sifted icing sugar.

DIPLOMAT CAKE

Metric	Ingredient	Imperial
170 g	orange marmalade	1 1/3 cups
85 g	dark rum	2/3 cup
	3 pkg ladyfingers	
128 g	heavy cream, whipped	1 cup
	Chocolate curls	

Method

1. **Line a 1-1/2-quart decorative** mold with plastic film.

2. **In small bowl, combine** orange marmalade with 1/3 cup rum; mix well. Set aside 1/4 cup of mixture, and refrigerate for later use.

3. **Split ladyfingers; brush cut** sides with remaining 1/3 cup rum. In bottom of mold, arrange two layers of split ladyfingers, cut side up. Spread with 2 tablespoons marmalade mixture.

4. **Around side of mold,** arrange a row of split lady- fingers, vertically, rounded side against mold. Continue layering ladyfingers and marmalade mixture to fill center of mold, ending with ladyfingers. Cover top with plastic film; refrigerate several hours or overnight.

5. **To Unmold, remove plastic** film from top; invert mold onto serving plate; gently remove mold and film. Spoon reserved 1/4 cup marmalade-rum mixture over top of cake, letting it drizzle down sides.

6. **Using pastry tube with** number-5 star tip, make rosettes of whipped cream around base of cake and on top. Arrange chocolate curls on top of rosettes. Refrigerate.

FESTIVE CHRISTMAS PUDDING

Metric	Ingredient	Imperial
225 g	golden caster sugar	8 oz
225 g	vegetarian suet	8 oz
340 g	sultanas	12 oz
340 g	raisins	12 oz
225 g	currants	8 oz
110 g	candied peel, chopped	4 oz
110 g	plain flour	4 oz
110 g	fresh white breadcrumbs	4 oz
55 g	flaked almonds	2 oz
	1 lemon, zest only	
	5 eggs, beaten	
	1 level tsp ground cinnamon	
	1 level tsp mixed spice	
	1 level tsp freshly grated nutmeg	
	pinch of salt	
150 ml	brandy or rum	5 fl oz

Method

1. Lightly grease 4x600ml/1 pint or 2x1.2 litre/2 pint pudding basins. Mix together all the dry ingredients. Stir in the eggs and brandy and mix well.

2. Spoon the mix into basins. Put a circle of baking parchment and foil over the top of each basin and tie securely with string. Make a string handle from one side of the basin to the other so it is easier to pick the basin out of the pan after cooking.

3. Put the basins in a large steamer of boiling water and cover with a lid. Boil for 5-6 hours, topping the boiling water up from time to time, if necessary. If you do not have a steamer, put the basins in a large pan on inverted saucers on the base. Pour in boiling water to come a third of the way up the sides of the pudding bowls. Cover and steam as before.

4. Cool. Change the baking parchment and foil covers for fresh ones and tie up as before. Store in a cool cupboard until Christmas Day. To serve: steam for 2 hours and serve with brandy butter, rum sauce, cream or homemade custard.

FOLAR CAKE

Metric	Ingredient	Imperial	Metric	Ingredient	Imperial
250 g	all purpose flour	2 cups	30 - 60 ml	hot water	1/8-1/4 cup
	7 tbsps butter softened + 6 spoons reserved for rolling			spice seasoning	
	2 1/2 tbsps dry active yeast			4 tbsp brown sugar	
	8 tbsps granulated sugar			2 tbsp ground cinnamon	
128 g	warm milk	1 cup		1 tbsp anise seed	
	1 tbsp fresh lemon rind			(folar finishing)	
	1 tsp salt			6 tbsp brown sugar	
	2 tbsp anise seed			2 tbsp canola oil	
				2 hard boiled eggs in shell	

Method

1. **Warm half of milk,** then add dry active yeast and blend, add some of measured flour, salt and blend to make a soft ball. Leave in bowl, covered with a tea towel and place in a warm draft free spot for 20min where it will double in size.

2. **Make tea with water** and anise seed, keep warm and set aside.

3. **After 20 minutes the** yeast and dough mix should have doubled. When ready, place remaining flour in large bowl, add sugar, remaining milk, flour yeast mixture, lemon rind and butter. Mix well and knead, dough will be a bit rough, slowly add splashes of warm tea with seeds, and continue kneading and adding splashes of tea until dough is soft and has lots of elasticity, approx. 20min. Leave to rise for an hour.

5. **While dough is rising** prepare pots, spice blend, heat oven and grease counter. When risen, remove half and gently spread into a rectangle on greased counter, try to keep the thickness uniform. Spread a thin layer of softened butter over entire surface then sprinkle generously with spice blend. Then fold half lengthwise towards center, spread butter and sprinkle with more spice mixture, do the same with the other half. Once both sides have been folded over spread butter over center and sprinkle again.

7. **Start at one end** and roll the dough onto and over itself until it looks like a chubby rolled bun, immediately place one of the rolled sides up in pan. Repeat with remaining dough.

9. **Bake Folars for 45** minutes at 200 ° C/400 ° F/Gas Mark 6.

KARPATKA CAKE

Metric	Ingredient	Imperial
125 g	Sweet Butter	1 cup
125 g	Flour	1 cup
	1 tbsp Baking Powder	
	4 Eggs	
	(for cake filling)	
470 ml	Milk	1 pint
125 g	Sugar	1 cup
	2 tbsp Potato Starch	
	2 tbsp Flour	
250 g	Sweet Butter	2 cup
	1 tsp Vanilla Extract	

Method

1. **Combine together sweet butter,** water, flour, and baking powder in a saucepan.

2. **Boil the mixture for** 3 minutes and remove from heat. Add eggs, stirring continuously.

3. **Pour the batter in** two baking dishes.

4. **Bake the cake at** 180 º C/350 º F/Gas Mark 4 for 30 minutes or until a toothpick inserted in the center comes out clean.

5. **Pour milk in a** saucepan and keep it for boiling.

6. **Add sugar, flour and** potato starch to the milk and stir well. Add vanilla extract. Remove and cool the mixture.

7. **Add butter and mix** well. Line the filling between the cake layers and refrigerate the cake to set.

KEY LIME PIE

Metric	Ingredient	Imperial
200 g	chocolate digestive biscuits	7 oz
50 g	butter, melted	1 3/4 oz
325 g	can condensed milk	11 oz
	1 egg	
	5 limes, grated zest of 3 limes and juice of 5	
	1 lemon, juice only	
	ice cream, to serve	

Method

1. **Preheat the oven to** 200 ° C/400 ° F/Gas Mark 6. To make the pie base, pop the biscuits into a roomy plastic bag and secure at one end. Crush, with a rolling pin, until they resemble crumbs. Transfer the crumbs to a mixing bowl and add the melted butter. Stir well to combine.

2. **Tip the crumbs into** the base of a 22cm loose-bottomed cake tin, pressing down well with your hand.

3. **Lightly whisk the condensed** milk with the egg. Stir in the lime zest from 2 limes along with the lime and lemon juice.

4. **Pour this mixture onto** the biscuit base in the cake tin. Scatter over the remaining lime zest.

5. **Bake the pie for** about 10 minutes, until just beginning to firm-up. Cool slightly before chilling in the fridge.

6. **Remove the pie from** its tin and serve with ice cream.

KIWI CAKE

Metric	Ingredient	Imperial
260 g	plain flour	2 cups
	1 1/2 tsp baking powder	
	1 tsp bicarbonate of soda	
	1/2 tsp ground cinnamon	
125 g	butter or margarine	1 cup
	2 tbsp honey	
125 g	caster sugar	1 cup
95 g	kiwifruit, chopped	3/4 cup
	2 eggs, lightly beaten	
	(for the cream cheese frosting)	
250 g	cream cheese	2 cup
	2 tbsp caster sugar	
	Juice of 1 lemon	

Method

1. **Preheat oven to 150** ° C/300 ° F/Gas Mark 2 and lightly grease a 23 cm spring form pan and line base with paper.

2. **Sift flour, baking powder,** bicarbonate of soda and cinnamon in a bowl and set aside.

3. **Combine butter, honey and** sugar in a large bowl and beat until creamy. Add kiwifruit, eggs and sifted flour. Mix well.

4. **Spoon into the pan** and bake for 40-45 minutes until cooked or a skewer comes out clean.

5. **Stand for 10 minutes,** then cool on rack. Spread the top and sides with frosting and decorate with kiwi slices.

6. **For the cream cheese** frosting: Beat the cream cheese until smooth. Add caster sugar and the lemon juice and continue beating until smooth.

7. **Leave in refrigerator for** 30 minutes before spreading on cooled cake.

LEMON DRIZZLE CAKE

Metric	Ingredient	Imperial
225 g	unsalted butter, softened	8 oz
225 g	caster sugar	8 oz
	4 eggs	
	finely grated zest 1 lemon	
225 g	self-raising flour	8 oz
	(for the drizzle topping)	
	juice 1 1/2 lemon	
85 g	caster sugar	3 oz

Method

1. Heat oven to 180 ° C/350 ° F/Gas Mark 4.

2. Beat together the butter and sugar until pale and creamy, then add the eggs, one at a time, slowly mixing through. Sift in the flour, then add the lemon zest and mix until well combined.

3. Line a loaf tin (8 x 21cm) with greaseproof paper, then spoon in the mixture and level the top with a spoon.

4. Bake for 45-50 mins until a thin skewer inserted into the centre of the cake comes out clean. While the cake is cooling in its tin, mix together the lemon juice and sugar to make the drizzle.

5. Prick the warm cake all over with a skewer or fork, then pour over the drizzle - the juice will sink in and the sugar will form a lovely, crisp topping. Leave in the tin until completely cool, then remove and serve. Will keep in an airtight container for 3-4 days, or freeze for up to 1 month.

LEMON MOUSSE CAKE

Metric	Ingredient	Imperial
	2 packages whipped topping mix	
235 ml	milk	1 cup
	1 package lemon jello	
150 ml	boiling water	2/3 cup
	2 packages soft ladyfingers	
	2 tsp lemon zest	
	4 drops yellow food coloring	

Method

1. **At medium high speed** beat topping mix and milk until thickened; reserve.

2. **Stir jello mix into** water until dissloved; stir in ice cubes until dissolved. At medium speed, slowly beat jello mixture into topping mixture until combined.

4. **At medium high speed** beat until fluffy. Add lemon zest and food coloring; combine into mixture.

5. **Coat a 9 inch** springform pan with cooking spray. Line pan with split soft ladyfingers, sides and bottom. **spoon mixture into springform pan.**

6. **Cover with plastic; chill** for 2 hours or until set.

MANDARIN AND CRANBERRY FRUIT JELLY

Metric	Ingredient	Imperial
	2 small boxes strawberry jello	
128 g	sugar	1 cup
	1 bag cranberries, ground, chopped	
	1 bag walnuts, ground, chopped	
	1 can crushed pineapple	
	1 small can mandarin oranges	
700 ml	hot (boiled) water	3 cups

Method

1. **Mix Jello and sugar** in a 9 x 13" dish. Add boiled water and the juice of the crushed pineapple, stirring until Jello and sugar mixture is dissolved. Allow to cool.

2. **Add ground/chopped cranberries and** walnuts, crushed pineapple and mandarin oranges, mixing well.

3. Chill overnight.

MARBLE CAKE

Metric	Ingredient	Imperial
225 g	butter, softened	8 oz
225 g	caster sugar	8 oz
	4 eggs	
	3 tbsp milk	
	1 tsp vanilla extract	
	2 tbsp cocoa powder	

Method

1. **Heat oven to 180** ° C/350 ° F/Gas Mark 4. Grease a 20cm cake tin and line the bottom with a circle of greaseproof paper. If you want to make life easy, simply put all the ingredients (except the cocoa powder) into a food processor and whizz for 1-2 mins until smooth. If you prefer to mix by hand, beat the butter and sugar together, then add the eggs, one at a time, mixing well after each addition. Fold through the flour, milk and vanilla extract until the mixture is smooth.

2. **Divide the mixture between** 2 bowls. Stir the cocoa powder into the mixture in one of the bowls. Take 2 spoons and use them to dollop the chocolate and vanilla cake mixes into the tin alternately. When all the mixture has been used up (and if young kids are doing this, you'll need to ensure the base of the tin is fairly evenly covered), tap the bottom on your work surface to ensure that there aren't any air bubbles. Take a skewer and swirl it around the mixture in the tin a few times to create a marbled effect.

3. **Bake the cake for** 45-55 mins until a skewer inserted into the centre comes out clean. Turn out onto a cooling rack and leave to cool. Will keep for 3 days in an airtight container or freeze for up to 3 months.

MERINGUE WITH CARAMEL CREAM

Metric	Ingredient	Imperial
	2 egg whites	
115 g	caster sugar	4 oz
	1 tbsp strong, cold coffee	
	(for the caramel cream)	
250 g	caster sugar	9 oz
	Pinch of cream of tartar	
500 ml	warm double cream	17 oz

Method

1. **Pre-heat the oven to** 140 ° C/275 ° F/Gas Mark 1.

2. **Whisk the egg whites** in a clean bowl and add half the sugar. Keep whisking until the mixture is really thick and glossy.

3. **Gently fold in the** rest of the sugar and the coffee. Pipe little swirls on to a baking sheet lined with non-stick baking parchment.

4. **Dry in the oven** for 1 hour until hard and crispy. Turn off the oven and leave the meringues inside until cold.

5. **Make the caramel sauce.** Place the ingredients in a heavy-based saucepan, add 225ml cold water and stir.

6. **Place over a low** heat and stir gently until the sugar has dissolved. Be careful not to splash the sides of the pan as stray sugar crystals can lead to crystallisation.

7. **Have a cup of** cold water and a pastry brush ready and use this frequently to run around the sides of the saucepan to "wash down" any syrup that is drying into crystals. Once all the sugar has dissolved, stop stirring (this is key for caramelising to take place) and do not stir again until the caramel stage is reached. When the mixture starts to boil, raise the heat and boil gently for 40 minutes until it turns golden, then remove from the heat at once to prevent it darkening and turning bitter.

8. **Add 500ml warm double** cream to the cooked caramel, stirring rapidly until dissolved.

9. **Beat the caramel sauce** until really thick and use to join 2 of the meringues together, then dust with cocoa powder before serving.

MIMOSA CAKE

Metric	Ingredient	Imperial
	(for the dough)	
60 g	Potato flour	2 oz
60 g	Flour	2 oz
80 g	Sugar	3 oz
	2 Egg yolks	
40 g	Butter	1 1/2 oz
	1 tbsp Icing sugar	
	(for the filling)	
	4 Egg yolks	
70 g	Sugar	3 oz
50 g	Flour	2 oz
500 ml	Milk	17 fl oz
	1/2 tsp Vanilla	
50 g	Hazel Nuts	1 1/2 oz
500 ml	Cream	17 fl oz

Method

1. **Using a fork, whisk** the eggs and the sugar in a bowl until they are foamy and full. Sieve both the flour and potato flour and add them to the mixture, a little at a time, mixing with a wooden spoon. Melt the butter and add it to the mixture and put it into a greased and floured oven dish.

2. **Bake in a pre-heated** oven at 190 ° C/375 ° F/Gas Mark 5 for 30 minutes. Then remove it from the oven and let it cool. Prepare the custard. Put the yolks into a bowl together with the sugar. Mix well, sieve the flour and the vanilla and add. Pour the boiling milk slowly through a strainer without stopping to mix.

3. **Put the mixture into** a casserole and still stirring, bring it to a boil over a medium heat. Continue cooking with the lid off for 7 to 8 minutes, mixing every now and then. Remove it from the fire and added the chopped up hazel nuts. Mix everything well again. Let it cool. Whip the cream up and add it to the custard which you will keep in the refrigerator.

4. **Divide the cake into** 4 horizontal layers one whole and the others 20, 18 and 16 cm in diameter. Brush each layer with flavoured water, spread them with the custard using a spatula and put them one on top of another in decreasing order. Cover with the remaining custard; crumb the rest of the cake and spread it over the whole surface and make it stick pressing it down with your hands. Sprinkle lightly with icing sugar.

NAPOLEON CAKE

Metric	Ingredient	Imperial
2 kg	self-rising flour	5 3/4 lb
800 g	butter, room temperature	1 3/4 lb
400 g	white sugar	14 oz
	1 egg yolk	
	1 tbsp water	
	Raspberry jam	
	(for the cake)	
600 g	butter (room temperature)	1 1/3 lb
600 g	white sugar	1 1/3 lb
1 kg	self-rising flour	2 1/4 lb
	2 tbsp milk	
	1/2 tsp vanilla	
	2 eggs	
	Strawberry frosting	
	Shredded coconut	

Method

1. Cream butter and sugar. Blend egg yolk with water; mix with butter and sugar mixture. Blend in flour. Roll out very thin. Line a grease lamington tin with half of the pastry. Prick well and spread with a good layer of raspberry jam.

2. For the cake: Cream butter and sugar. Beat in eggs. Fold in flour, then milk and vanilla. Pour this mixture into the pasty case, making a slight hollow in the center. Roll out the remaining half of the pastry; spread with raspberry jam. Place on top of cake with jam side face down.

3. Bake in moderate oven 180 ° C/350 ° F/Gas Mark 4 for 35-40 minutes, or until pastry is browned and sponge cake is done. Turn onto a wire rack to cool. When cold frost with strawberry flavoured pink frosting, then sprinkle with shredded coconut.

PANETTONE

Metric	Ingredient	Imperial	Metric	Ingredient	Imperial
	1 tsp sugar			finely grated rind of 1/2 a lemon	
	1 tbsp dried yeast			finely grated rind of 1/2 an orange	
	4 tbsp milk		400 g	plain (all purpose) flour or white bread flour, sifted	14 oz
100 g	butter	4 oz			
50 g	caster sugar	2 oz		1 tsp salt	
	1 tsp vanilla extract		100 g	raisins or sultanas	4 oz
	3 (free range if possible) eggs, beaten		75 g	chopped mixed peel	3 oz

Method

1. **Preheat the oven to** 200 ° C/400 ° F/Gas Mark 6. Butter a 20cm (8 in) cake tin and line with lightly buttered greaseproof paper. Pour the milk (or buttermilk) into a bowl, then sprinkle on the sugar and yeast. Leave for around 10 minutes – it should start to go frothy.

2. **Combine the butter and** caster sugar in a bowl and beat them together until they are very fluffy. Then beat in the eggs gradually, followed by the lemon and orange rind (and the vanilla extract if you're using it).

3. **Place the flour and** salt in a large bowl. Now gently fold in the milky/yeast fluid, followed by the creamed butter/sugar mixture. Mix them all together until you have a soft dough. Put the dough onto a lightly floured surface and knead for about 5 minutes until it's smooth.

4. **Then place the dough** into an oiled plastic bag (or cover with a tea-towel and leave in a warm place). Leave it for about an hour until it has doubled in size.

5. **Sprinkle the raisins/sultanas and** mixed peel over the dough. Knead until they are completely mixed in. Place the mixture in the cake tin and leave it in a warm place, until it has doubled in size again. It will take about 45 minutes.

6. **When it has risen,** bake it in the oven for 10 minutes, then reduce the heat to 180 ° C/350 ° F/Gas Mark 4 and bake it for another 30 minutes. When it's done it should be golden brown and firm to the touch. Cool the panettone, and dust it with icing sugar.

PAVLOVA

Metric	Ingredient	Imperial
	4 egg whites	
225 g	golden caster sugar	8 oz
	1 tsp cornflour	
	1 tsp white wine vinegar	
	1/2 vanilla pod	
284 ml	carton double cream	9 1/2 fl oz
	1 lemon, zested	
450 g	berries, raspberries, strawberries, or blackberries or a mixture	16 oz
	1 tbsp icing sugar	

Method

1. **Heat the oven to** 180 °C/350 ° F/Gas Mark 4. Cover a baking sheet with baking parchment. Whisk the egg whites with electric beaters until they just form stiff and shiny peaks. Gradually add the sugar a couple of tablespoons at a time and whisk really well between each addition.

2. **When all of the** sugar is used up continue whisking for 3-4 minutes or until the meringue is stiff and glossy and stands up in peaks, then whisk in the cornflour and vinegar. Spoon the mixture onto the baking parchment and use a palette knife to make a circle about 20cm in diameter. Put in the oven, turn the temperature down to 120C/fan 100C/gas 1/2 and cook for 11/2 hours. Turn the oven off and leave the meringue inside until completely cold (you can make this the day before and leave to cool overnight).

3. **Carefully peel off the** baking parchment and put the pavlova on a serving dish. Don't worry if it cracks. Scrape the vanilla seeds into a mixing bowl, add the cream and lemon zest and softly whip, then spoon onto the pavlova. Mix the berries, spoon the fruit on top of the cream, dust with a little icing sugar and serve.

PEACH CAKE

Metric	Ingredient	Imperial
	2 tbsp butter	
32 g	brown sugar	1/4 cup
	canned or fresh peaches	
170 g	Tea Biscuit mix	1 1/3 cups
96 g	sugar	3/4 cup
	3 tbsp soft shortening	
	1 egg	
177 ml	milk	3/4 cup
	1 tsp vanilla	

Method

1. **Melt butter in 8** inch square or 9 inch round cake pan. Sprinkle with brown sugar.

2. **Arrange fruit on top** of butter and sugar. Mix biscuit mix and sugar. Cut in shortening. Blend well.

3. **Add egg and a** third of the milk. Beat vigorously for 1 minute. Gradually stir in remaining milk, and vanilla.

4. **Beat 1/2 minute. Pour** cake mixture over fruit. Bake 35 to 40 minutes at 180 º C/350 º F/Gas Mark 4.

5. **Invert at once on** serving plate. Cool slightly and remove pan.

PEACH PIE

Metric	Ingredient	Imperial
	3 Egg Whites	
130 g	Granulated Sugar	1 cup
	14 Saltine Crackers, finely crushed	
	1 tsp Vanilla Extract	
	1/4 tsp Baking Powder	
65 g	Pecans, chopped	1/2 cup
	7 Fresh Peaches, peeled, pitted and sliced	
260 g	Sweetened Whipped Cream	2 cups

Method

1. **Preheat the oven to** 170 ° C/325 ° F/Gas Mark 3.

2. **Whip the egg whites** in a large glass bowl until they hold a stiff peak. Sprinkle the sugar in gradually, continually whipping the egg whites.

3. **Fold in the crushed** saltine crackers, pecans, baking powder and vanilla.

4. **Spread the mixture evenly** into an ungreased 9 inch deep dish pie plate. Bake for 30 minutes, or until a toothpick inserted into the center comes out clean.

5. **Remove the pie from** the ovenand allow to cool completely.

6. **When the crust has** cooled completely, place the sliced peaches evenly over the top.

7. **Cover the pie with** aluminum foil to avoid browning.

8. **When ready to serve,** evenly top with whipped cream.

POUND CAKE

Metric	Ingredient	Imperial
385 g	granulated sugar	3 cups
230 g	unsalted butter	1/2 lb
	5 eggs shopping list	
385 g	all-purpose flour	3 cups
	1 tsp salt	
130 g	buttermilk	1 cup
	1/4 tsp soda dissolved in 1 tbsp hot water	
	2 tsp quality vanilla	

Method

1. Cream butter and sugar well

2. Add eggs, one at a time, beating well after each addition

3. Add flour (sifted with salt) alternately with buttermilk

4. Add soda/hot water mixture

5. Beat well, add vanilla

6. Pour into greased and floured tube pan and bake 1 hour and 20 minutes at 300 ° C/150 ° F/Gas Mark 2.

PROFITEROLES

Metric	Ingredient	Imperial	Metric	Ingredient	Imperial
	(for the choux pastry)		600 ml	double cream	1 pint
200 ml	cold water	7 fl oz		1 tbsp icing sugar	
	1/2 tsp caster sugar			(for the chocolate sauce)	
85 g	unsalted butter	3 oz	15 g	butter	1/2 oz
	pinch salt			4 tbsp water	
115 g	plain flour	4 oz	175 g	good quality plain chocolate, broken into pieces	6 oz
	4 medium eggs, beaten				
	(for the cream filling)				

Method

1. **Preheat the oven to** 200 ° C/400 ° F/Gas Mark 6.

2. **To make the pastry,** place the butter, water and sugar into a large saucepan. Place over a low heat to melt the butter. Increase the heat and shoot in the flour and salt all in one go. Remove from the heat and quickly beat the mixture vigorously until a smooth paste is formed, stirring continuously to dry out the paste. Once the paste curls away from the side of the pan, transfer the mixture into a large bowl and leave to cool for 10-15 minutes.

3. **Beat in the eggs,** a little at a time, stirring vigorously until the paste is smooth and glossy. Continue adding the egg until you have a soft dropping consistency. It may not be necessary to add all the egg. The mixture will be shiny and smooth and will fall reluctantly from a spoon if it is given a sharp jerk.

4. **Lightly oil a large** baking tray. Dip a teaspoon into some warm water and spoon out a teaspoon of the profiterole mixture. Rub the top of the mixture with a wet finger and spoon on to the baking tray. This ensures a crisper topping. Bake for 25-30 minutes, until golden brown, if too pale they will become soggy when cool.

5. **Remove from the oven** and prick the base of each profiterole. Place onto the baking tray with the hole facing upwards and return to the oven for 5 minutes. The warm air from the oven helps to dry the middle of the profiteroles.

6. **Prepare the filling: lightly** whip the cream and icing sugar until soft peaks form. Do not overwhip. When the profiteroles are cold, using a piping bag with a plain nozzle, pipe the cream into the holes of the profiteroles. If a piping bag is not available cut the profiteroles in half and spoon in the cream with a teaspoon.

7. **Prepare the chocolate sauce:** melt the chocolate with the water and butter over a pan of boiling water. Stir without boiling until smooth and shiny. Arrange the buns on a serving dish and pour over the hot sauce. Eat hot or cold.

RAISIN CAKE

Metric	Ingredient	Imperial
130 g	raisins	1 cup
260 g	water	2 cups
65 g	butter	1/2 cup
	1 tsp baking soda	
	1/2 tsp salt	
130 g	white sugar	1 cup
	1/2 tsp ground cinnamon	
	1/2 tsp ground nutmeg	
130 g	chopped walnuts	1 cup
225 g	all-purpose flour	1 3/4 cups

Method

1. **Preheat oven to 180 ° C/ 350 ° F/ Gas Mark 4.** Lightly grease one 10 x 10 inch baking pan.

2. **In a large saucepan** boil the raising with the water for 10 minutes. Add the butter or margarine and let cool.

3. **In the same pan** add the flour, soda, salt, sugar, cinnamon, nutmeg, and chopped nuts (optional), mix well and pour batter into a lightly greased 10x10 inch baking pan

4. **Bake for 35 minutes.**

RASPBERRY CHEESECAKE

Metric	Ingredient	Imperial
	8 digestive biscuits	
50 g	butter, melted	1 3/4 oz
600 g	cream cheese	21 oz
	2 tbsp plain flour	
175 g	caster sugar	6 oz
	vanilla extract	
	2 eggs, plus 1 yolk	
142 ml	pot soured cream	5 fl oz
300 g	raspberries	10 1/2 oz
	icing sugar	

Method

1. Heat the oven to 180 ° C/350 ° F/Gas Mark 4. Crush the biscuits in a food processor (or put in a plastic bag and bash with a rolling pin). Mix with the butter. Press into a 20cm springform tin and bake for 5 minutes, then cool.

2. Beat the cream cheese with the flour, sugar, a few drops of vanilla, eggs, the yolk and soured cream until light and fluffy. Stir in half the raspberries and pour into the tin. Bake for 40 minutes and then check, it should be set but slightly wobbly in the centre. Leave in the tin to cool.

3. Keep a few raspberries for the top and put the rest in a pan with 1 tbsp icing sugar. Heat until juicy and then squash with a fork. Push through a sieve. Serve the cheescake with the raspberry sauce and raspberries.

RHUBARB PIE

Metric	Ingredient	Imperial
	(for the pastry)	
225 g	butter	8 oz
55 g	caster sugar	2 oz
	2 eggs, preferably free range	
340 g	white flour, preferably unbleached	12 oz
	(for the filling)	
750 g	red rhubarb, sliced about 1cm(1/2in) thick	1 1/2 lb
250-400 g	sugar	9 oz-14 oz

Method

1. **Preheat the oven to** 180 ° C/350 ° F/Gas Mark 4.

2. **First make the pastry.** Cream the butter and sugar together by hand or in a food mixer (no need to over cream).

3. **Add the eggs and** beat for several minutes. Reduce speed and mix in the flour.

4. **Turn out onto a** piece of floured greaseproof paper, flatten into a round wrap and chill. This pastry needs to be chilled for at least 1 hour otherwise it is difficult to handle.

5. **To make the tart,** roll out the pastry 3mm/1/8in thick approximately and use about 2/3rds of it to line a 21.5cm/8 3/4in square x 2.5cm/1in deep with fluted edge tin.

6. **Lay the rhubarb in** the pastry base and sprinkle with the sugar.

7. **Cover with a lid** of pastry, seal edges, decorate with pastry leaves, brush with the egg wash and bake in the preheated oven until the rhubarb is tender, approximately 45 minutes to 1 hour (but do keep checking some ovens may vary cooking time).

SIMNEL CAKE

Metric	Ingredient	Imperial	Metric	Ingredient	Imperial
	(for the almond paste)			Pinch salt	
250 g	caster sugar	9 oz		1/2 tsp ground mixed spice	
250 g	ground almonds	9 oz	350 g	mixed raisins, currants and sultanas	12 oz
	2 free-range eggs, beaten		55 g	chopped mixed peel	2 oz
	1 tsp almond essence			1/2 lemon, grated zest only	
	(for the cake)			1-2 tbsp apricot jam	
175 g	butter or margarine	6 oz		1 free-range egg, beaten for glazing	
175 g	soft brown sugar	6 oz			
	3 free-range eggs, beaten				
175 g	plain flour	6 oz			

Method

1. **For the almond paste,** place the sugar and ground almonds in a bowl. Add enough beaten egg and mix to a fairly soft consistency. Add the almond essence and knead for one minute until the paste is smooth and pliable.

2. **Roll out a third** of the almond paste to make a circle 18cm/7in in diameter and reserve the remainder for the cake topping. Preheat oven to 140 ° C/275 ° F/Gas Mark 1. Grease and line a 18cm/7in cake tin.

3. **For the cake, cream** the butter and sugar together until pale and fluffy. Gradually beat in the eggs until well incorporated and then sift in the flour, salt and mixed spice (if using) a little at a time. Finally, add the mixed dried fruit, peel and grated lemon zest and stir into the mixture. Put half the mixture into a greased and lined 18cm/7in cake tin. Smooth the top and cover with the circle of almond paste. Add the rest of the cake mixture and smooth the top leaving a slight dip in the centre to allow for the cake to rise. Bake in the preheated oven for 1 3/4 hours. Test by inserting a skewer in the middle - if it comes out clean, it is ready. Once baked, remove from the oven and set aside to cool on a wire rack.

4. **Brush the top of** the cooled cake with the apricot jam. Divide the remainder of the almond paste in half; roll out a circle to cover the top of the cake with one half and form 11 small balls with the other half. Place the circle of paste on the jam glaze and set the balls round the edge. Brush the cake topping with a little beaten egg.

5. **Preheat the grill to** high. Place the cake onto a baking tray and grill for 1-2 minutes, or until the top of the marzipan begins to brown. Alternatively, lightly heat the cake topping using a cook's blow torch, until the marzipan is golden-brown.

STICKY TOFFEE PUDDING

Metric	Ingredient	Imperial	Metric	Ingredient	Imperial
	(for the pudding)			2 free-range eggs	
90 g	butter, softened	3 oz	200 g	self-raising flour	7 oz
30 g	plain flour	1 oz		1 tsp bicarbonate of soda	
200 g	dried dates, pits removed	7 oz		(for the sauce)	
300 ml	water	10 3/4 fl oz	100 ml	double cream	3 1/2 fl oz
170 g	dark brown sugar	6 oz	40 g	butter	1 1/2 oz
	1 tbsp golden syrup		40 g	dark brown sugar	1 1/2 oz
	2 tbsp black treacle			2 tbsp black treacle	
	1/2 tsp vanilla extract			1 tbsp golden syrup	

Method

1. **For the pudding, preheat** the oven to 200 ° C/400 ° F/Gas Mark 6. Butter the pudding basins really well with a third of the softened butter, then dust with the plain flour.

2. **Place the dates and** the water in a saucepan and bring to the boil.

3. **Whisk the remaining butter** and the sugar together in a large bowl using an electric beater until light and fluffy. Gradually add the golden syrup, treacle, vanilla extract and eggs to the mixture and continue beating. Turn the beaters down to a slow speed and add the self-raising flour, a spoon at a time. Beat until all the ingredients are well combined.

4. **Purée the hot water** and date mixture in a food processor or blender and add the bicarbonate of soda. Quickly add this to the mixture in the bowl while it is still hot. Stir to combine and fill two or three 7.5cm/3in metal pudding basins (or one 12.5cm/5in pudding basin) with the mixture.

5. **Bake in the oven** for 20-25 minutes until the top is just firm to the touch.

6. **For the sauce, place** all the sauce ingredients into a pan and bring to the boil. Remove from the heat.

7. **To serve, remove the** puddings from the moulds and put on a serving plate with lots of the hot sauce on the top. Serve with ice cream.

TARTE TATIN

Metric	Ingredient	Imperial
	(for the pastry)	
320 g	plain flour	11 oz
225 g	ice-cold butter	8 oz
110 g	icing sugar	4 oz
	3 free-range egg yolks	
	(for the filling)	
	6 Cox or 4 Granny Smith apples, peeled, cored and cut into 8-12 wedges	
	1/4 lemon	
110 g	caster sugar	4 oz
110 g	butter	4 oz

Method

1. Preheat the oven to 250 ° C/500 ° F/Gas Mark 9.

2. First, make the pastry. In a food processor, mix the flour, butter and icing sugar just until they resemble breadcrumbs. Add the egg yolks and, using the pulse button, mix until it comes together in a dough. Remove the dough from the mixer bowl and divide into two pieces. Wrap in clingfilm and put in the freezer to chill for at least an hour.

3. For the filling, place the apple wedges in a bowl, squeeze the lemon juice over them and toss them gently. Sprinkle 85g/3oz of the sugar in a heavy-bottomed pan and place on the hob over a medium heat, turning the pan frequently and making sure the sugar doesn't burn. Allow the sugar to caramelise a little and become a pale golden brown, then remove from the heat and arrange the drained apple pieces in one layer over the bottom of the pan.

4. Place the pan in the oven and bake until the apples have softened a bit and started to release some liquid - about 10 minutes. Remove from the oven and sprinkle over the remaining sugar and dot the butter on top. Remove the pastry from the freezer and, using the coarse side of a cheese grater, grate the pastry with long steady strokes over the apples until it forms an even layer at least 2.5cm/1 inch thick. Do not press down. Return to the oven, turn the heat down to 220 ° C/425 ° F/Gas Mark 7 and bake until the pastry is golden brown - about 20 minutes. Remove from the oven and leave to rest for a minute or two.

5. Take a heatproof serving dish that is generously larger than the pan on all sides and place over the pan. Protecting your hands with a dry folded tea-towel, and holding the dish and pan firmly together, quickly and carefully flip the pan and the dish so that the pan is on top. Tap the pan sharply a few times all round with a wooden spoon, then lift off. The tart should be left on the serving dish with the apple on top.

TIRAMISU

Metric	Ingredient	Imperial
250 g	mascarpone	9 oz
	1 tsp vanilla extract	
	3 tbsp Marsala, brandy or Tia Maria	
150 ml	strong coffee or espresso, cooled to room temperature	5 oz
150 ml	single cream	5 oz
	4 tbsp icing sugar	
	16 sponge fingers (savoiardi)	
	Frozen bar of 70% of chocolate bar	
	Cocoa powder, to dust	

Method

1. **Whisk the mascarpone with** the vanilla and Marsala and 50ml coffee, until everything is thoroughly mixed together. Whisk the cream with the icing sugar until smooth, then fold in the mascarpone mix

2. **Pour the remaining coffee** into a bowl (sweeten with more icing sugar if you like). Take one sponge finger at a time and dip it in to the coffee. Set it to one side and continue with the remaining biscuits

3. **Line 4 serving glasses** with 4 sponge fingers, breaking them in half if you need to. Spoon the mascarpone mix in until you reach the top of the glass. Refrigerate for 20 minutes to allow the flavours to infuse.

4. **Remove the tiramisu from** the fridge. Take the frozen chocolate bar and grate a little chocolate over the top of each Tiramisu. Finally, dust with sifted cocoa powder to serve.

TRADITIONAL FESTIVE FRUIT CAKE

Metric	Ingredient	Imperial	Metric	Ingredient	Imperial
225 g	plain flour	8 oz	100 g	chopped mixed peel	3 1/2 oz
	1/4 tsp salt		150 g	glacé cherries, halved	5 oz
	1/2 tsp mixed spice		100 g	blanched almonds, chopped	3 1/2 oz
	1/2 tsp ground cinnamon			brandy	
200 g	butter	7 oz		(to decorate the cake)	
200 g	dark brown sugar	7 oz	200 g	marzipan	7 oz
	2 tbsp black treacle			1-2 tbsp apricot jam, warmed	
	1 tbsp marmalade			royal Icing	
	1/4 tsp vanilla essence			3 free-range egg whites	
	4 free-range eggs, lightly beaten		600 g	icing sugar, sieved	1 lb 5oz
				2tsp liquid glycerine	
800 g	mixed dried fruits	1 3/4 lb		1 tbsp lemon juice	

Method

1. **Heat the oven to** 150 ° C/300 ° F/Gas Mark 2. Grease a 20cm/8inch round or an 18cm/7inch square cake tin and line the bottom and sides with baking parchment. Sieve the flour, salt, mixed spice and cinnamon into a bowl. Cream the butter and the sugar in a large mixing bowl and then mix in the sugar, treacle, marmalade and vanilla essence until light and fluffy.

2. **Mix the eggs a** little at a time into the mixture adding a tablespoon of flour mixture with the last amount. Fold in the remaining flour mixture until well mixed and then mix in the dried fruit, mixed peel, glace cherries and the almonds. Turn the mixture into the prepared tin and make a slight hollow in the centre.

3. **Bake in the oven** for 3 hours and then test with a skewer. If not ready bake for up to another hour testing every 20 minutes until the skewer comes out clean. Remove from the oven and leave to cool in the tin for 15 minutes. Turn out on to a wire rack and leave to cool. Once cool, make a few holes in the cake with a skewer and pour over 3-4 tbspof brandy. Let the brandy soak into the cake. Store the cake wrapped in foil and in an airtight tin or plastic container, holes side up.

5. **To decorate the cake,** place the cake on a foil board or cake plate. Dust your hands and the work surface with a little icing sugar and knead the marzipan until soft. Roll out half the marzipan to fit the top of the cake and roll out the rest in strips to fit around the sides of the cake. Brush the cake all over with the warmed apricot jam and then place the marzipan on top and around the cake.

6. **Cover the cake with** a clean tea towel and then leave in a cool place for at least one day. To make the icing, lightly whisk the egg whites adding the sugar at intervals. Beat well until the icing reaches soft peaks. Add the glycerine if using and the lemon juice. Spread icing all over cake either flat iced using a clean ruler or by forming soft peaks. Decorate with Christmas ornaments.

TRIFLE

Metric	Ingredient	Imperial
	1 Swiss Roll, Victoria Sponge or Trifle Sponges	
	1 packet Strawberry or Raspberry Jelly	
	Strawberries or Raspberry (tinned, frozen or fresh)	
600 ml	Home-Made Custard, cooled	20 fl oz
150 ml	Cream Sherry	5 fl oz
	Strawberry or Raspberry Jam	
	Toasted Flaked Almonds	

Method

1. **Slice the swiss roll,** (if using victoria or trifle sponges, spread with a little jam). Arrange in the bottom of a glass serving bowl.

2. **Pour the sherry over** the swiss roll or sponges. Add the fruit.

3. **Prepare the jelly as** per the instructions (if using tinned fruit use the juices). Pour the jelly over the fruit and sponge.

4. **Place in the refrigerator** and allow to set. Pour custard over jelly.

5. **Whisk the cream and** spread or pipe on the top of the custard.

6. **Decorate with almonds.**

TSOUREKI

Metric	Ingredient	Imperial
	3 cakes of compressed yeast	
120 ml	lukewarm water	1/2 cup
1 kg	flour	8 cups
	1 tsp of sugar	
235 ml	condensed milk	1 cup
190 g	sugar	1 1/2 cups
225 g	unsalted butter or margarine	1/2 pound
	grated peel of 1 lemon	
	1 tsp of sea salt	
	2 eggs, whisked	
	4 egg yolks, whisked	
	1 egg, whisked	
	sesame seeds or blanched sliced almonds (optional)	

Method

1. **Dissolve yeast in lukewarm** water. In a mixing bowl, combine 1 cup of flour, 1 teaspoon of sugar, and the yeast in water and beat well to mix, creating a smooth batter. Cover tightly (with a close fitting cover or plastic wrap) and set aside in a warm place for 30 minutes to rise.

2. **In a large saucepan,** combine condensed milk, butter or margarine, sugar, and grated lemon peel, and heat to lukewarm. Add yeast/flour mixture, salt, 2 whisked eggs, whisked egg yolks, and stir well.

3. **Transfer to a large** bowl and add flour slowly, to create a soft dough. Knead for about 15-20 minutes by hand on a floured surface (or 10 minutes with a mixer). Cover and allow to rise in a warm place until doubled in bulk, about 1 hour 30 minutes.

4. **Punch the dough down,** knead for a few minutes, and form into three loaves. Place loaves on greased cookie sheets or baking pans, cover with clean kitchen towels, and set in a warm place to rise until doubled in size, about 1 hour. Preheat oven to 175 ° C/ 350°F/ Gas Mark 4.

5. **Using a pastry brush,** brush loaves with beaten egg. (Optional: Sprinkle with sugar, sesame seeds, or blanched almond slices.) Bake for 30 minutes or until golden brown. (Tap on the bottom; loaves should sound hollow.) Cool on racks.

TWO LAYERS PLUM CAKE

Metric	Ingredient	Imperial
225 g	self-raising flour	8 oz
	1 tsp ground cinnamon	
100 g	baking margarine	3 1/2 oz
50 g	sultanas	2 oz
50 g	soft brown sugar plus 2 tbsp for sprinkling	2 oz
	2 large eggs	
	4 tbsp golden syrup	
225 g	plums, stoned and chopped	8 oz

Method

1. **Preheat oven to 160** ° C/325 ° F/Gas Mark 3.

2. **Grease and line an** 8 inch square baking tin.

3. **Rub the flour, half** the cinnamon and the margarine together.

4. **Add the sultanas and** 50g (2oz) brown sugar and stir.

5. **Beat eggs and syrup** together in a separate bowl, add plums, then stir into flour mixture. Transfer to tin and level surface.

6. **Mix rest of brown** sugar and cinnamon and sprinkle over top of cake mixture.

7. **Cook in centre of** oven for 45-50 mins and then test. It should be risen and just firm to the touch when cooked.

8. **Cut into squares to** eat.

UPSIDE DOWN PEAR CAKE

Metric	Ingredient	Imperial
	2 tbsp butter	
32 g	light or dark corn syrup	1/4 cup
32 g	brown sugar	1/4 cup
	6 pear halves, cooked or canned	
64 g	walnut or pecan halves	1/2 cup
43 g	shortening	1/3 cup
64 g	granulated sugar	1/2 cup
	1 beaten egg	
85 g	molasses	2/3 cup
260 g	all-purpose flour	2 cups
	1/2 tsp salt	
	2 tsp baking powder	
	1/4 tsp baking soda	
	1 tsp cinnamon	
	2 tsp ground ginger	
175 ml	sour milk (add 2 tsp vinegar to cup then add milk)	3/4 cup

Method

1. **Melt butter in a** 9-inch round cake pan. Blend syrup and brown sugar; add to pan. Fill pear halves with pecan halves; place in the pan wide sections towards center, to make a star-like design.

2. **In a large mixing** bowl, cream butter and sugar; beat in egg. Add molasses; beat well. Add sifted dry ingredients alternately with milk, beating on low speed until smooth. Pour batter over the pears. Bake at 190 ° C/ 350° F/ Gas Mark 4 for 55 to 65 minutes, or until a wooden pick or cake tester inserted in center comes out clean.

WALNUT APPLE CAKE

Metric	Ingredient	Imperial
250 g	plain flour	8 oz
	2 tsp ground cinnamon	
	1 tsp bicarbonate of soda	
	1/2 tsp salt	
300 g	caster sugar	10 oz
	1 tsp vanilla extract	
	3 tbsp water	
200 ml	light oil	
	3 eggs, lightly beaten	
	3 apples, peeled, cored and quartered	
125 g	chopped walnuts	4 oz

Method

1. **Pre-heat oven to 190** ° C / 375 ° F / Gas mark 5. Grease a 9 inch / 23cm cake tin.

2. **Sift together the flour,** cinnamon, bicarbonate of soda and salt.

3. **Add in sugar, vanilla,** water, oil and eggs; mix until well-blended.

4. **Stir in apple quarters** and chopped walnuts.

5. **Pour into tin and** bake for 50 minutes or until a knife inserted into the middle comes out clean.

6. **Cool on a wire** rack before serving.